The Fog *of the* Midnight Hours

G.M. Manzi

Raw Earth Ink

2023

This book is a work of poetry.

First paperback edition April 2023

ISBN 979-8-98660-526-5 (paperback)

Published by Raw Earth Ink
PO Box 39332
Ninilchik, AK 99639
www.raw-earth-ink.com

For Jess,
who saw me at my lowest,
and decided to guide me through it anyway.

"I'm forgiving everything that forgiveness will allow and there's nothing I can do about it now."
                                                    -Willie Nelson

"Forget your personal tragedy. We are all bitched from the start and you especially have to hurt like hell before you can write seriously."
                                                    -Ernest Hemingway

"But since it falls into my lot that I should rise and you should not, I'll gently rise and softly call goodnight and joy be with you all."
                                                    -Scottish folk song

Preface

Hemingway is quoted as saying that the only thing to writing is to "sit down at a typewriter and bleed." This is the truest writing advice there is (that and what Bradbury says about going to college for writing, which you shouldn't). All Hemingway was saying was *write honestly*. But what *is* honest writing, exactly? We could sit here and debate that question all day. Contrary to popular belief, honesty in writing doesn't always walk hand in hand with truth. Sure, a good ninety percent of us draw from real world experiences, the people we've known, and conversations we've had. But that's where the actual fabric of reality stops and our version of the truth begins. Fiction writers are not historians or biographers. We are observers, and our job is to bring to the reader our dressed-up interpretation of what we see, hear and experience in such a way that you, the reader, can and hopefully will create your own interpretation of *our* interpretation.

That's *this* writer's goal, anyway. In the preface of my first book, *We Lived Like Kings,* I noted that I follow Chekhov's lead and not hold your hand as you read. Not all writers follow that, of course, and I'm not saying my way is **the** be-all, end-all.

When *does* honesty come into play, you might be wondering, after I just stated this is all my interpretation of the truth of what I saw, see, and hear. The honesty part, for me, is more symbolic than it is literal, because it comes from within. The heart and the soul and the gut. It's opening yourself and exposing all of the vulnerability you're too afraid to expose in real life. You bleed out your traumas and your heartaches and your disappointments and your sadnesses just as much as you reveal your joys, kinks, past, and what makes you *you*—all to give your interpretation of the truth for a reading public that may or may not give a shit that you just bled to death in front of a typewriter. You can always tell as you read something if the author died a little while putting ink to paper, and when they're just pretending they did.

Many writers, even though we may dabble in fiction, are the most honest people you'll meet, and sometimes the most courageous. It isn't easy to pick the scabs of scars left by deaths or chronic depression or sexual assault or betrayals. Nor is it easy to write fully about someone you love, or to reveal a long hidden secret that you know there's no coming back from. Once we open that lid, there's no stuffing it back into Pandora's Box.

This book you hold in your hands took a lot out of me. Not every piece did. Some were simply from some bullshit thought I had. Some I wrote while drunk or stoned and didn't see them until the next day where they were met with a resounding *what in the fuck is this?* But, boy, there are those I had to walk away from before coming back to finish. Those which made me angry, hateful, or sad beyond description all over again to recall and interpret the truths as I felt, saw, and experienced. Some I won't be able to read again for a while — but in the end it all made for a stronger book.

Why write, then, some might ask. The answer, for me, makes complete sense — it comes easy to me, so I do it and I love doing it. I want you to laugh and cry and get mad right along with me. I hope you enjoy the ride as much as the ride pained me, at times, to make it go. I bleed at the typewriter so you can live vicariously through the reality of experience. It's what virtual reality wishes it could be. Love it, or hate it, we writers and creative types just hope by the end of it you appreciate all that bleeding we do.

A lot of hurt and regrets were poured into this one, but on a personal level, writing this was a time of intense personal growth. I learned how to let go, move on, and accept things without a looming fear of defeat. You hold in your hands a little piece of myself and a testament to my growing pains. A sacrifice for the sake of escapism and entertainment.

— G.M.M.
Albany, New York — 2023

Crumbs in My Chest Hair

I eat from a bag of pretzels at two in
the morning alone and drunk in my bed.
An empty bottle of red table wine lies empty on the floor.
Crumbs and salt fall onto my bare chest,
where I either brush them off onto my sheets,
or leave them lost in the dense forest of
chest hair until my next shower.

I was supposed to have company tonight
but that didn't pan out.
And if it had?
I probably would not be about to finish an
entire bag of Rold Gold sourdoughs to soak up the
bottle of cheap table red I polished off in roughly an hour.

Fuck it, what do I care if there's crumbs in my
chest hair and crushed into my sheets?
It's my bed and my chest hair, after all.
I don't care a lick

I should though,
and perhaps that's the reason
why there's no company tonight.

Rotting on the Serengeti

What sort of sick and twisted buzzard have I become?

Catered lunch from the Manager's Meeting earlier is
left over in the conference room,
lying out in the open like a zebra carcass
rotting on the Serengeti.

I stand in the doorway, mouth frothing and drooling spittle,
with a gaze in my eyes which is more beast than man,
grateful for the Master's scraps.

I ravenously rummage through foil trays of meatballs,
sausage and peppers, and baked ziti that have been
warming for hours on steam heat, piling my plate high before
seating myself to devour my feast.
You'd think it was my first solid meal in days.

I feel disgusting.
I feel ashamed,
I no longer feel hungry.

Writing and Shitting

For the first hour or two of my workday,
I try to write.
Any little stupid thought I have will get jotted down and
either expanded on then, or at a later date.

I'll sometimes do this for the last hour or
two of my day as well,
depending on how busy I am.
It helps take my mind off of the
repetitive, trivial, completely mindless tasks that I am
all too aware a baboon could do.

If I can't write, I try to shit.
More than once a day, too, if I'm bored.
If I'm mind numbingly bored and time
drags on at an agonizingly slow pace,
I'll just sit in the stall for five to twenty minutes.
Shitting on the clock is one of the few
times I feel I've beaten The Man at his own game.

If I don't shit, I try to write,
and so on and so forth and what have you.
If I can do neither?
I'm in for a long day.

This is what my life has come to —
basing the quality of my day on whether or
not I can write or shit on the company dime.

Zigged Rather Than Zagged

If there's one thing I want you to
take away about me when all is
said and done it's this —

That despite every dumb thing I've ever done,
every bad decision made,
every chance blown and opportunity wasted,

every person I upset, hurt, let down,
disappointed, and made curse having had known me,

every time I zigged rather than zagged and
ducked when I should have looked —

I was just trying like hell to do the right thing.
Right by me,
right by you,
right by everyone I know and knew.

Even if it doesn't look like I did, I was.
I promise.
I tried like hell.
I tried my best.

When I knew it would never be enough,
and when I knew it might cost me dearly,
I damn well tried my best.

There wasn't any other choice.

Every Hour on the Hour

He looked over from his recliner to the clock on the wall that
loomed over him like the chaplain that escorts the condemned.

>*Nine-thirty*, he thought to himself, defeated,
>*Off to bed soon,*
>*and it was such a nice weekend too. Fuck.*

He did not get up to move to the bed.
Instead he remained seated.
Sadness washed over him.
A great, overwhelming wave of sadness that
was soon followed by an equally large wave of dread.

>*All those applications*, he thought to himself,
>*all those interviews this past month – they went nowhere.*
>*Meaningless. Fucking meaningless.*

After roughly ten minutes he finally rose and walked,
shuffled rather, like a sad old man sixty years his senior,
towards his bed.
He stared at the unmade bedding and
a terrible numbness overtook him to the
point he thought he felt his knees buckle.

He finally got undressed and laid down,
and stared at the ceiling in sorrow before shutting his eyes.

>*I swear*, he said aloud to nothing but empty space,
>*At the rate I'm going the only way I'll escape this job is when I*
>*escape this life.*

He hardly slept. He had a nightmare that was
nothing more than a bad day at work.
No monsters. No death. Just a bad day.
He then proceeded to wake up every hour on the hour,
for the next six hours,
until his alarm went off at four-thirty,
and the week could begin fresh and new.

He didn't have it in him to even turn the alarm off.
Instead, he wept.
It then occurred to him he was out of
sick days, and he wept some more.

First Entry

The very first entry he wrote in his brand
spankin' new leather bound journal was the following —

*The woman who gave this to you on your
birthday may just be the love of your life,
try not to be an idiot and forget that.*

She turned out to not be the love of his life,
but rather, one of his saddest heartbreaks.
He would make a mistake she tried to forgive but couldn't,
and not for his lack of trying to redeem himself.
There was also a fifty-fifty chance
she got back at him for it in the
worst way he could imagine.

But the journal was nice,
almost too nice for him,
and nothing bad had happened yet.

Try as he might,
and he could never bring himself
to throw it out afterwards.

The Fog of the Midnight Hours

They walked arm in arm down the all but
deserted downtown streets, just after midnight.
A cold mist hung in the air, giving the
streetlights and neon bar signs a subdued, ghostly glow.
This was the old part of the city, where there
were still cobblestone streets and antique domed
streetlights left over from the city's Gilded Age splendor.
Hassam could've painted the scene.

He walked as slowly as possible, trying to not
give away to her that he doing so purposely.

They eventually arrived at the cab her friends had
gone ahead to grab and piled into, waiting for her.
The sounds of the Saturday night
revelers faded into the dark and damp of night.

The two of them hugged one more time before she got in.
It was a full embrace, tight and strong, but comforting.
Familiar.
It was left unspoken but they knew they'd
never meet again, and they wanted it to mean something.

> *You're a good person*, she whispered into his ear,
> *And I sincerely enjoyed having this time with you tonight.*

They pulled away, the slight wetness he
saw gathering in her eyes was proof of her sincerity.

> *Thank you*, was all he could think to say,
> and she understood why he could say no more.

She smiled a melancholic smile,
then proceeded to brush his shoulders with both hands before
patting down and straightening the lapels of his coat.
She leaned in and kissed him, affectionately, on the cheek.
Her lips felt cold and otherworldly,
and he didn't know if it was due to the amount
of Guinness he had drank that night,

but he found himself comforted rather than put off by this,
as there was a tenderness from her that passed through him.

Their gaze met as she pulled away,
her eyes, aqua green earlier, now appeared, he believed,
spectral grey,
but like her lips, the tenderness of her eyes, too, was
otherworldly.
He saw in them what he felt to be the vastness of
some great beyond that existed well outside the
grasp of what he knew and understood.
A place whose existence as well as its
inhabitants he was forbidden to know
until it was his turn and he was called.

Her melancholic smile remained as she finally
turned to get in and join her friends to their next destination.
The cab pulled away, and she disappeared back
into the mist and mystery of the night,
as if she were one with all its secrets.

He hoped to take away from this something deep,
some meaning or lesson from this experience.
The only thing he knew for certain was that as
quickly as she came into his life,
she was now gone from it.

He rubbed his cheek with his hand,
he thought he could still feel her lips there,
but when he closed his eyes she was no longer there.
Some paths, he knew, were not meant to intersect twice.
Some mysteries exist to remain unsolved,
and the stories we are in are oftentimes not our stories at all.

>*Three hours*, he said to himself as he put his
>cold hands back into his coat pockets,
>*Three drunken hours out of a*
>*lifetime — and I'll never know what the hell for.*

As he turned from where he stood and began walking back,

he found himself wishing he could remain behind in
the fog of the midnight hours and be one with its
riddles and its increasingly biting cold,
rather than return to the light and warmth of the
blissfully ignorant living, which he believed
held nothing for him anymore.

Nothing like having touched and known the unknown,
as he had, for three drunken hours out of a lifetime.

The Dream of Dreams

I am extraordinarily lucky today,
work is slower than hell and I have no
tasks to keep me overly busy today and
that means I may not even break a sweat.

I am okay with that.
I am at peace with that.
I have resigned myself to and
have accepted that.

I pray today continues at one menial task an hour —
a phone call here, a filed document there,
while I sit here at my desk on the
warehouse floor and listen to Bach.

Boy, wouldn't that be the dream of dreams?
To sit in a climate controlled office with the
door closed on a ninety-five degree day while
listening to *Cello Suite 1 in G Major* as
I catch a nap while nobody's looking?
Maybe build a really cool fort underneath my desk.

Sounds marvelous, doesn't it?
Just positively marvelous.

That I, Like Marley

She's done well for herself and I'm
genuinely happy for her.
She deserved better than me anyway, much better.
I was a worthless shit back then---
dumb and immature and selfish.
I had quite a bit of growing up to do,
and with that came the painful truths
that only come with hindsight.

I wish I could tell her that I *did* love her,
and I'll forever be sorry that I
wasn't then how I am now.

But that'll never happen,
and it appears that life would
rather I wear this chain of guilt around my
neck that I, like Marley, forged in life like
the self absorbed fool that I was.

Clinging

I never tell anyone what my greatest fear is —

That becoming the person that did all the right things,
took all the right steps, worked harder than hell,
persisted and did his due diligence,
and tried terribly to remain positive only
to watch as day after day passed without
ever being able to say *I got my shot.*

The chance that never came,
never even being in the cards.
That terrifies me more than anything on God's green Earth —
dying while clinging to the chance that never came.

I never tell anyone my greatest fear,
It's simpler just to say spiders.

With Twenty on the Horizon

You and I are no longer close,
and haven't been for years.

We never speak,
and I have no interest in your life,
much like you've none in mine.

Don't take offense to that though,
because whenever I think of my life then,
years ago, nineteen years old with twenty on
the horizon and away from home without a
care or worry in my heart,
I always find you there.

I will always find you there.

Escape to the Open Ocean

Most of my coworkers are just out of high school;
we're talking between seventeen and nineteen being the
average.
Being in my thirties makes me geezer-in-residence,
but we all get along because I treat them like
adults and they all agree I neither look nor
act my age, whatever the hell that means.

I was like them once, when I was an eighteen-
year-old dishwasher at the local diner,
wondering where the hell the thirty- and
forty-year-olds were doing waitressing or
short-order cooking, laughing silently to myself,
not spitefully, but arrogantly,
my youthful pride believing that'd never be me.

I'm one hundred percent sure most,
if not all, wonder what the hell
a college educated dude in his thirties is
doing chopping jalapenos and,
in an all too sobering moment of "never say never,"
scrubbing pots and pans in the local *Chipotles*.
How'd this sorry fuck screw up? I'm sure they wonder.
I'm with you guys. I thought the same
about Bobby Clark and Jenny Beebe when
I was fresh-faced and ready to conquer the world.

As long as they don't find me creepy, they
can think whatever they want.

Those free-spirited little fuckers,
how I envy them so.

I envy their humor,
which has yet to turn bitter.
I envy their excitement for the future,
which has yet to become a stress riddled present.
I envy the carefree shine in their eyes that

life and all its trials and hurdles has
yet to beat from them, dulling the glimmer.

I like them all, they make me laugh and
sometimes even forget my own bitterness,
and I'm reminded too that I still have bit of
life left in front me yet.

I can tell which girls will blossom by the time
they're twenty-five, and which fellas are
destined to be stand up, honest men of wit and honor.

It kills me that not all of them will go places or
are destined for great things.
Some are destined for a crap life they couldn't avoid.
Some are destined to be entitled, suburban soccer moms.
Some are destined to become trash.
Some are destined to be like me —
starting over in their mid-thirties at
a *Chipotle* after a few misguided decisions.

But, like the newborn sea turtle,
a few will escape the bloodbath and
escape to the open ocean.

Promise me you'll make better decisions than I did,
guys, promise me you'll at least try.
I'd hate for you to become like me or worse.

-For all my 2018-2020 *Chipotle* coworkers
Audentes fortuna iuvat

One of Two Ways

The way I see it, honey,
this could go one of two ways —

The first —

You finally grow up and
we share a pint of Guinness and a joint on
the porch the way we should have by now,
and we go on living happily like
we never had any bumps in the road.

Or,
the second —

I forget you exist and the sole memory
of you is that you were an attention whore and
a flake that never achieved her true potential and
I drink and smoke on
the porch by myself.

It's your move,
I've made enough moves already
for the two of us.

Dance With Me

Only this do I kindly ask of you —

> To take my hand with no fear,
>   to be the darkness that ends my days,
>   and to dance with me amongst
>   the wicked mists and shadows
>   the dance of the witching hour.

Here, Now, and Forever

Dear Lord,
I really don't ask all that
much of you often,
so please,
hear and answer my prayer —

> Here, now and forever,
> Oh Lord,
> grant me the strength to
> still give a shit about those that
> don't give a shit that
> I give a shit about them.
>   — Amen.

Morphine Drip

I don't have time for this.

The words echoed cold and sharp in his mind.
A dagger to the heart that
both numbed and nauseated him,

I don't have time for this.

This is what she, his friend,
had told him late at night when,
needing just a little time for a helping hand,
he had told her, in a moment of self pity and despair,
that he wished his heart would beat slower and
slower until it stopped that night.

He didn't mean it, but damn it,
he needed a hand, a shoulder,
a friend, someone to give a damn
for all of ten minutes.

I don't have time for this –
annoyance was what he got instead.

Rage came to him,
blinding in its intensity –

Attention whore!
Fat ass bitch!
Indifferent slut!
Selfish cunt!

Then he heard the dial tone on the other end,
and he felt a complete and total numbness.
The morphine drip of a dying man.

I don't have time for this, he said aloud to himself,
before he laughed and cried and laughed and cried
and laughed and....

What He Needed to Hear

She was passing from his mind,
and he knew there was nothing that
could be done about it.

He could remember that her eyes were
deep and gentle, but he had forgotten
whether they were hazel, caramel, or dark brown.

He thinks that her lips made him
helpless with one kiss but,
why did they?

He's certain her body was both
fair and soft of skin and
thickset with a solid build,
but, was it really?

He was sure her laugh was
full and hearty but,
he may be mistaking it
for somebody else's.

Even her scent had begun to fade.
The essence of spring rain in late March,
and the sharp crispness of recently melted snow.
The one thing he prayed for every
night since she left was to keep
that scent always on his mind and at the
ready to pick out of thin air on a moment's notice.

It was a rare prayer answered,
and one, in the long run,
we wished would not have been.

Fresh as the day you were born,
he would tell her when they hugged
tight and he buried his face in her
long dark hair which rested on her shoulder,
and she would giggle playfully before

kissing him tenderly,
and his entire body trembled in helpless reverence.

Now he remembers.
Now it comes back, not just her scent,
but all of her,
and it's so overwhelming that
he finds he cannot physically stand.

He is not overjoyed,
like he believed he would be.
What his body feels is trembling anxiety,
what his soul feels is sorrow,
what his heart feels is anguish,

and he thought then and there,
for the first time, that feeling nothing
would be for him a blessing.

He fought back the lump in his throat,
he must be steady, he must steel himself,
if tears came, he knew he'd never say what
he needed to hear himself say —

Now is the time to say goodbye.

Forgotten in a Sea of Dunes

This was his worst nightmare.
This was going make him curse and cry and
tailspin and reignite his darkest hate and
self-loathing and self-doubt and most agonizing sadness
But it needed to be done.
He knew he'd probably put this off for far too long as it was.

It needs to be done, he told himself,
and he had hoped that the currency in pain it would cost
would contribute to buying himself a better tomorrow.

But, he said, God damn it,
it didn't need to be this way, did it?

All you had to was confirm or deny but,
you didn't do that did you?
What you did instead was ignore and
cut me off completely and what it did was
cost me what little I had left of my dignity and self respect.
The bitch of it is up to that point we were on
pretty pleasant terms, and had spoken, pleasantly too,
not three days prior, remember?
You even asked how things were going with the new
girlfriend.

Let me remind you of what happened.
The day you chose to ignore me and in your
act of doing nothing say Fuck you to me was
when I texted you, at six in the morning,
after I read the message that worthless,
cowardly shitbag sent me an hour earlier.

I woke up to this shit,
and it sent me into anxiety riddle convulsions —

Hey faggot I fucked Linda too just so you know.
She sucked my dick once at the house
and I watched her kiss you after.

No way this could be true.
I had to ask you,
because obviously I didn't believe it.
How could I?
Why would I?

> *Hey so Shitbag is telling me that you*
> *guys fucked and there was a time that*
> *you sucked his dick while we were all at the house,*
> *there's no truth to this right?*

Right?

I don't know.
I will never know.
You were supposed to respond with a
What the fuck of course I didn't.
Maybe even with a little rage at the very idea I would believe
that.

You never responded, though,
and you never would.
I'd never hear from you again, actually,
and I'll never be sure that you *did* fuck one
of the people who was,
at one time, closest to me.
In your silence there is truth.
In your silence there is admission of guilt.
In your silence, there could also be nothing,
but I have to assume, forever now,
that it's all very true even if it isn't.

I would have rather have been told yes.
I would rather you had liver punched me then and
let me battle through the wrath and rage and
inconsolable sadness that no doubt would've
come over me than live with the silence you gave.

It didn't end there though,
I became obsessed.

Ahab chasing the white whale.
I *had* to know the truth.
I texted, and called, and emailed,
and texted, and called, and emailed.
Then I realized that my number was blocked,
adding even more fuel to the bonfire of sad, sad suspicion.
I became hellbent.
Tunnel vision.
I emailed, and emailed, and emailed,
and emailed and emailed and cried and emailed more.

For a full calendar year I did this,
seeking answers to a terrible question I should
never of had to ask, knowing in the back of my
mind it was hopeless and I would never get my answer.
Stuck now, am I, with an open wound that
will likely never heal.

God damn you to hell,
do you know what that did to me?
Do you have *any* idea at all what that did to me?!
Christ almighty, do you care?

Nervous tremors that my shrink confirmed were
anxiety attacks, which I had never had before.
Sleepless nights, so many sleepless nights.
My work being affected by my moodiness and
my head being elsewhere.
Mood swings and rage directed at the few
people left that loved me and were trying to help.

The emasculation, the complete emasculation,
from knowing there's a very real possibility you
really did have your way with that scumbag's dick.
It castrated me and murdered my libido.
My desire to fuck essentially died,
arousal became a thing of the past.
I questioned myself as a man,
and the two of you fucking being all I could
think about almost ruined things with the saint that

I call my current lady
(but it didn't, and God bless her soul
for loving a schmo like me).

You gave me nothing.
Nothing but silence and cowardice.
Four years we shared together.
May as well be a fart in the wind or
piss in a flowing stream.
We were friends, too, after we ended.
I understand I wasn't perfect,
that I made a mistake or two in those four
years but, did I really deserve *this?*

I loved you. So much.
I really, truly did.
Now?
Now the thought of you makes me want to hurl,
and every memory I have of you is poisoned.
I'm left feeling hateful, nauseated, and sad beyond
words at the mere mention of your name.
Admitting to even *that* is painful.
I'd hope to never talk about or
think about you this way.
Not ever, but here we are or at least,
here I am.

Everything about you, every memory that
made me smile and warmed my heart is a
cancer that must now be aggressively cut out and discarded.
Burned to ashes, and then instead of being
cast into the wind to become one with the universe I
instead flush them like a useless dead goldfish.
I need to say a goodbye.
A very hard goodbye.
The hardest goodbye to a living
person that I've ever had to make.
A solemn funeral with no hopeful sermon,
no wild Irish wake to celebrate what was,

and no pipers to play for you *Amazing Grace* and *Danny Boy*.

<u>I</u>

Our first date—we met at Dave and Busters, an attractive plus sized girl in a black puffer jacket, black leggings, and black boots. I liked you immediately. I had a Newcastle to drink, you a vodka-soda. We played a couple rounds of air hockey before you said you could go for some nachos and you mentioned how you liked the way *Chili's* made them so I drove us down the road to *Chili's* where we shared a giant nacho platter and bits and pieces of our lives and ourselves. How I was just trying to find my way and how you were aspiring for your Masters in psychiatry and maybe even your PhD, and you let me hold your hand and I couldn't believe how smooth it was and you giggled a little when I said that. Your laugh, your smile, your mind—it was all melting me. It had been three years since I had a date this good, and longer since I felt my heart begin to melt. I concluded this was one of the, if not the, best first dates I had ever had, which I shared with you, and you agreed. Before we got back in my car I gifted you something you had mentioned loving in a passing conversation, before we agreed to meet and were feeling each other out, which was a box of cherry Pop Tarts. Cherry was your flavor of choice, and it led to me buying you cherry cola, cherry vodka, cherry candy, cherry everything over the next few years—that was our little inside joke. That box of Pop Tarts led to our first kiss, you kissed differently than all the others that came before and I felt it in my bones that you were different.

We made out a little in my car as a February snow began to fall. I looked at you and said how I didn't want the night to end, and you agreed with me and I asked if you'd like to follow me back home where I lived. It was not lust that drove me but the sincere desire to spend as much time with you as humanly possible. You trusted me and agreed to follow. Sex did not come that night but we explored each other's bodies and I concluded I loved the naked body you were self

conscious about and we fell asleep pretty contented. We knew there was more come. Early as it was, it felt like you would be the one to pull me from the alcohol fueled black hole of self pity and loathing I had been living in. For the first time in a long time, I knew I had something to look forward to.

-Goodbye.

II

My first birthday you spent with me. After watching me guzzle my body weight in beer you drove me back to that massive loft apartment you lived in at the time with that massive claw foot tub in the bathroom. You made me for the first time your seven layer bean dip and we both destroyed it in less than an hour as we watched *Supernatural* before making love, but I was way too drunk and bloated with beer and beans and chips and we didn't get very far. Next morning I woke up to your lips around my cock to make up for the previous evening, which was followed by you making me French toast and even though you didn't drink coffee your roommate did and you had a full pot ready to go. Your hair hung down and covered your shoulders and your smile as you poured my coffee was the sweetest thing I had seen in years and was a better birthday gift than sex or two inch thick French toast or seven layer bean dip at one in the morning could ever hope to be.

-Goodbye.

III

The night you drank too much 'cause even though you hardly ever drank you wanted to drink what I was having so I made you a 7n7 stupidly thinking you could handle that but you were more a vodka and rum drinker and didn't like whiskey and we both erroneously thought eating a box of Superpretzel at eleven at night would help soak up the booze but instead you vomited into a plastic garbage bag so hard you burst the blood vessels in both your eyes and you legitimately

looked like a demon for about three days. I laughed pretty hard about that even if it did scare the bejesus out of me the next morning. You didn't drink so much as a wine cooler for about four months after that.

-Goodbye.

IV

The way you dressed. Fall and winter were your best seasons to show off your fashion sense. You always dressed understated yet classy and chic. Tall and thickly built with a well endowed chest, wide hips, thick legs and ass—you never showed off but you instead let the imagination tell the story because you knew damn well how much I enjoyed undressing you with my eyes. Always a black or navy sweater or long sleeve shirt, black boots of varying material and style, and either black leggings or black, grey, or red plaid skirt and black or navy or sometimes dark brown stockings (that was my favorite). Your hair, long and thick and dark brown with a few blonde streaks, always fell down along the shoulders of your wool sweater and the skirt and stockings showed off your legs and what you used to joke as your juicy ass. Your understated ability to dress in layers was your sexiest ability.

As good as you would become in bed once you gained a little more confidence in yourself, watching you undress was the real treat and I would replay it over and over in my head even after we had long since ceased glistening as a couple. The sweater came first, followed by the tank top you always layered with, then the bra (always black or navy colored), revealing your D-sized chest. The boots came next, followed by the skirt, leaving you naked save for the tights. I loved seeing you stand there in just your black tights from waist to heel, You knew I loved it, and you loved knowing that I loved it. Your dark eyes would look at me invitingly. Coyly. That's when I'd pull you close and kiss you deep, and run my hands along the smooth nylon on your ass and legs. Then finally they too would be off followed lastly by your panties. It felt like unwrapping a present on Christmas and never being

disappointed. I loved seeing you stand there in the dim light of my bedroom naked next to the pile of clothes you just shed. A real woman. How lucky I felt. How blessed I was.

-Go to Hell.

V

As a love maker you weren't fancy or wild or burning with passion's white-hot heat. You were shy, almost timid, but once you became more and more comfortable you loosened up and that became less of an issue. Your skin was soft and smooth from bare neck to bare heels. I remember on our first or second date you for some reason told me that you prided yourself on your smooth skin and its complexion and how you hated to be dry anywhere and how you even used the foot scraper to get the dead skin off the bottom and I said that's a hell of a thing to say during dinner and you defended it like a child defending the existence of Santa and said *Trust me it makes a difference* and I thought 'whatever' 'cause I had never cared or noticed that in another woman before and you sure were right about it and while I'm nowhere near a foot fetishist your heels, ankles, and inner arches were smooth as caramel and I didn't mind kissing them occasionally while your legs were in the air. Your hair always fell over your neck, shoulders, and face in an alluring manner. Your full and pouty lips knew how to kiss and you had the strongest, most surprisingly forceful tongue I thought existed.

You never came during sex and I tried to never take it personally. It didn't matter though, because I knew the way to make you climax was through your clit and you knew what it meant when I would slyly whisper into your ear *Ready for a rub?* And it would take roughly five minutes of gently using my middle finger on you to send you into convulsions that would sometimes border on violent thrashing and it was beautiful. For someone who had such an unassuming attitude in her day-to-day, you sure sucked like a champ and knew precisely what to do to me every time to make my eyes roll back which they did every time and the first time you allowed

your mouth to take my climax was momentous because for so long you were adamant you never would and when you did I knew you had accepted me. You loved being plowed from behind, as you always put it, and again for someone with such an unassuming attitude you sure did love getting your thick ass covered once I hit the precipice.

There was nothing disgusting or explicit or extreme to our time in the bedroom. That didn't make it any less special. You transitioned me to adult lovemaking and I have to stop talking about this right now because I feel a nervous tremor coming on.

-God fucking damn you for making me do this.

VI

Going to the haunted house with my sister. I always found it odd that you, someone who loved both fall and Halloween, got scared so easily, and hated watching horror movies at any point in time. Anyway the both of you were terrified and I was laughing my fool head off until I left you both behind and ran for my life when that random hand came shooting out of the dark to grab me in what can only be described as some sort of laboratory with holding cells and body parts everywhere like some Nazi torture dungeon. I could hear the two of you in the distance calling me a son of a bitch and I had zero shame that night of being a coward and choosing flight over anything else—which is sort of what you've done to me.

-Fuck you.

Thanksgivings at your house where I felt warm and welcome and comforted listening to you pray and say grace. Blessing us with good health and happiness for years to come as your leg was wrapped around mine under the dining room table. I looked at you after the Amen and smiled and you smiled shyly knowing this was my first time seeing you in this setting and being spiritual and liking this side of you.

-Fuck you.

35

When you had caught and confronted me for being far too overly flirtatious with someone for far too long and made me realize how completely terrible and nauseating it is to be completely in the wrong and knowing that I had been a scumbag despite my having no malicious intent. This was the first time in my life I was forced to confront the fact that yes there was something wrong with me and you got me to finally admit I should see a therapist.

I sobbed. That's all I could think to do. Then I begged and you kept your distance, not even sitting on the same couch as me, and I was afraid to even say anything because those dark eyes that were always soft and loving were suddenly cold and hard and it terrified me. I knew I had done wrong and I promised to do whatever it took and I felt like a piece of shit because how many other men in the world had done worse than I did and not cared about having done it but had still said that very same thing to a broken-hearted angel? Was I no better than them now?

We sat on the couch in silence for a moment and I couldn't look at you because of the shame I felt and you couldn't look at me because you felt betrayed and I thought to myself *Well this is it* until I very faintly felt your hand rest on top of mine and you softly squeezed it and I cried and softly squeezed it back. We sat there like that for fifteen minutes.

-I am forever sorry.

Seeing the Mormon Tabernacle Choir for free through your church. You looked good that summer night, and they put on a hell of a performance and I finally got to see and more importantly hear what all the fuss was about MOTAB. This was shortly after our hard spell, and I was trying very hard to come back into your good graces and I could still feel your tension and apprehension and mistrust towards me.

You held my hand the entire show. I thought we'd be okay.

-Fuck you.

The day we were bored and decided to visit the Yankee Candle factory two hours away. We didn't buy anything but you did get me the apple butter I saw there a few months later for Christmas and we bought the same exact gummy candy sharks they sold there at the gas station down the road for half the price Yankee was asking before having a massive supper at Cracker Barrel. I'll always regret not having our caricatures drawn up.

-I hate you.

The food we'd eat together. You liked when I'd make gourmet burgers on pretzel buns and my egg sammies in the morning and drunk nachos in my bed watching *Seinfeld* and that banana cream pie you made me the last birthday you spent with me.

-Fuck you.

VII

The very last time I saw you. The July after I first moved into my new place. We hadn't seen each other in maybe two years since the rather sad fizzle of a breakup we had but we had been speaking regularly again and were once again friendly and laughing and bantering. I picked you up after you dropped your car off at the shop and we went to grab breakfast before I showed you the new digs. I didn't expect to make love during that visit but we did for the first time since the breakup and you made me cum so hard I thought I'd break and then I asked about ten minutes later when I got my breath back if you were ready for a rub and you replied with a smile that of course you were and I rubbed you until you too almost came so hard you broke.

Holding your hand the entire ride back to the mechanic's, the way you'd look over to smile at me, it sure felt that we were on our way back to where we never should've left in the first place. That we were healed or damn near close to healing and that you really were about to turn that corner with me and become the forever woman I had always believed you should have been.

-God damn you God damn you God damn you.

VIII

You're the first woman that not only listened to Tom Waits with me, but thoroughly and sincerely enjoyed him. Mainly his first two albums *Closing Time* and *Heart of Saturday Night* primarily because we both preferred the piano jazz sound to his weird Vaudeville-sounding latter day works.

Tom almost played a major role in our lives too which I'm sure you completely forgot. Three years in and we were serious as hell, we had, I thought, moved on from my stupidity and were stronger than ever and you basically lived at my place because you couldn't stand living in that house with your absent-minded father and your mother who always passed awful judgment on you and at this point we'd have those lovely pillow talks naked late at night or out at a quiet and intimate dinner and we'd discuss what our first dance song would be at the wedding which I feel all optimistic couples do at one point in time or another. We got on the topic of weddings and first dances because I remember I had said something along the lines of how if or when we got hitched we'd have a bitchin' wedding or at least a bitchin' reception and we'd be one hell of a power duo and I asked what you thought for our first dance. You thought about it for a moment before looking at me with a wry smile and said *For us? How about Tom Waits?*

My heart jumped up into my throat and I couldn't believe that you---this beautiful, classy woman suggested dancing in front of her strict Mormon family to Tom Waits. I loved it. I could have kissed you and I think I may have before asking what song and you said after some more thought *Ol' 55?* and I definitely kissed you after that. From that point forward, *Ol' 55* belonged to you and me and no one else and I

would dream about and think about and imagine the two of us dancing on that very special day to a very special song meant only for you and me.

-Go to Hell. Go to fucking Hell.

IX

The last Saturday before Christmas doing some last minute shopping. I wish it were the shopping that I say goodbye to but no. No that just wouldn't be special enough. That just wouldn't hurt nearly enough. No. It just has to be one of my, if not my favorite, thing you and I ever did together. This was after my fuckup and still during the healing process. After you had slowly begun trusting me again but still fell into bouts of tense apprehension. It was hard at times. Very hard. But we were trying.

We were leaving the big Target up by the suburbs where I joked only the Beautiful People shop. You had gotten my dad a few movies I told you he might like and I snuck a bag of Luden's cough drops for you as a gag gift because still to this day (and this is something else I hope to say goodbye to is this fact) you're the only person I've ever known to always have a bag of them on your person all the time and would snack on them at the movies or at the house like they were Jolly Ranchers and I made fun of you saying you were like Mr. Pitt eating a Snickers with a knife and fork in the *Seinfeld* episode where Jerry gets a woman's number off the Aids Walk list and fuck you for making me say goodbye to having *Seinfeld* marathons together. Back to the Luden's. I know you loved them 'cause they were cherry, your favorite flavor. Another thing I have to say goodbye to. Fucking bitch.

We were leaving Target and you weren't heading back to the highway and when I asked where we were going you pinched my cheek and mockingly told me *It's gonna be a SUPWISE!* like I was four years old and this annoyed me 'cause it was nine thirty at night and I was tired after a long day amongst the crowded insane holiday masses and wanted us to get home and comfy as soon as possible and when I protested you laughed it off and told me to quit being such a baby. I was annoyed and you knew it 'cause I had told you many times I hate being suckered into plans I don't account for like whenever I'd help my buddy Steve move some furniture he insisted would only take two hours next thing you know I'm across town with him four hours later recycling scrap metal for his cousin Barry.

You just let me sit there and pout like a sulking child who didn't get everything on his Christmas list and you just sat there driving with a shit-eating grin on that lovely little face. Then we entered the suburbs where the Beautiful People actually live, in a neighborhood I could only ever dream of living in, and I finally asked what the fuck we were doing. Then you told me to shut up and look ahead. And I did. And it was about the loveliest God damn thing I ever did see and I ceased immediately being annoyed and grouchy.

There in front of me, every Tony Soprano-looking palace on the hills was aglow with the most elaborate, dreamy, wondrous display of Christmas lights I had ever seen. The beauty was beyond description. I was transfixed. You drove slowly and I sensed you looking over at me but I couldn't look back because I was too busy being wowed but what I was seeing and I felt your free hand rest on my thigh and gently squeeze it. Everywhere you looked — walkways, porches, doorways, garages doors, the rooftops, all along the gutter line, in bushes and trees and around elaborate Romanesque columns — lights, lights, and more lights. Reds and blues and whites and yellows. Some strung vertical, some horizontal, some in elaborate patterns and shapes. One immaculate, palatial house that I can only imagine was housing the tree from Rockefeller Center had a massive wreath on its main door, and all the windows facing the street and we're talking maybe a dozen windows had candles lit and resting in the center of them it was straight out of Dickens.

Every single house was decorated and lit up. Not a

single house as bare of Yuletide cheer and if God looked down from high and saw the landscape lit up from his seat in the clouds, illuminating the season's joy he would have decreed that this is good. I don't know for how long we drove around there. You took your time and I was glad that you did. At some point I finally looked over at you. Your eyes were on the road, your head periodically moving to glance at this house here and that house there. Your hair was tied back in a loose ponytail and the collar of your down puffer jacket was still up. You finally looked over at me and smiled and it was your genuine and happy smile because when you *were* genuinely happy your eyes would become a squint and you finally asked if I was still annoyed with you and I said not at all. And looking at you illuminated by the soft and dreamy glow of blue and purple and green and yellow I never thought you had ever looked more beautiful or tender as you did in that moment, and I asked you to stop the car and you did and you knew why because when you did you leaned in and kissed me gently and lovingly and passionately and I never wanted that moment to end and then you looked right at me after and said very softly that you loved me so much and that you were sorry for having been difficult, and I said I was sorry for having been a stupid piece of shit and that I loved you too and terribly at that and I thanked you for this wonderful surprise.

When we made love that night I could still see the glowing prism of lights in your eyes.
 -God damn you. God fucking damn you.

X

Your scent. Fuck you. God damn it. So we've come to it at last: your scent. My favorite thing in the world about you, the last part of you to linger on and, admittedly, what I've hung onto for far, far too long. The scent that made me helpless, weak in the knees, at your beck and call, putty in your hands. That's all it took to make me yours and you smelled like that from the first day I met you to the last day I saw you. The mists off a cascading waterfall. A forest creek after a spring

rain. April dewdrops on my face every time I'd hug you and bury my face in the nape of your neck where your hair fell and I'd inhale like all of life and existence depended on it. I would feel reinvigorated and alive again as I'd exhale all of Life's misery and strife. I wanted to bottle it like well-water and drink deep from it during a mid-July heat wave. I told you every single time that you were as fresh as the day you were born and every time you'd giggle with glee over it. It made me feel unburdened and untroubled and FUCK YOU I CAN'T DO THIS ANYMORE!

> A quick and unforeseen dull, numbing pain
> was felt in his chest, which was accompanied
> by the heavy pull of heartache,
> causing him to pause and wince.
> His fingers stopped running the keys,
> and he pulled his hands away from the keyboard.

> Tears came earlier but this was worse.
> This pain was every fiber of his being reminding him
> that there would be no closure,
> and no going back from this.
> Briefly he saw her smile, heard her laugh,
> felt her touch, tasted her lips, and smelled her scent.
> His heart, already broken, was doing the crying for him,
> and he knew his work must continue through to its finish.

I hope,

> he began again, hoping all his sadness and anger and
> despair and regret would be felt with every word,

that you and he both rot in the deepest,
darkest pits of Hell for making me wipe this all from my
mind and I'm going to pray to God that I never go
back to revisit any of this and that the part of me that wants to
love you again dies and stays entombed.
That you stay as distant and faded a memory to me as
playing tag in first grade recess — where I know it
was part of my life even though I don't remember ever doing it.

A face without a voice, a body I can't feel and a
scent that will blow away and lose itself like
so many grains of sand forgotten in a sea of dunes.
I pray on bended knee to forget all that made you *you*,
and everything that made us *us*.
I pray to be rid of your ghostly hold on
my memory and my life and what remains of it on my heart.

Please leave.
I beg you, please leave and stay gone unless
it's to resurface and confess and apologize and
pay penance for helping to damage me to my very core—
mind, body, and soul.

No.
Stay gone, it's better this way.
There's no telling what damage the system shock from
seeing or hearing from you might cause,
and how fucking sad is *that*.

You can't fade away fast enough.
I don't even want to curse or hate you anymore,
I just want this, *need* this, to end,
to be gone, to no longer haunt me.
As I say all of this to you,
know that my beaten, battered heart has wailed in
agony with each word written,
and that it prays with me and holds my hand as
I say this one final time—

       I did truly love you.
       And to you, to us, to all that...

                  -Goodnight.

Better Than Nothing

I still,
to this very day,
believe in my heart of
hearts that it's
better to be someone's
regret than to have
been nothing at all.

Reflection

When I look at the
        reflection in the mirror,
with tired, dead eyes and
        a neck and face badly in
need of a trim,
        I no longer ask
Who are you, but rather —
        What the fuck
                have you become?

Power of Positivity

Hard to stay positive,
I always say,
when every decision you
ever made—

        The big, the small, the personal,
        the professional, the momentous,
        the insignificant, the life changing,
        and the small ones made daily...

                ...has felt like the wrong one.

Pig Roast

A few months ago I woke
suddenly from a dream I had where I
was at a big, riotous pig roast.
I hadn't been to a pig roast in years,
I thought, as I grabbed my water bottle off
the night stand and took deep gulps to rid
myself of the cotton mouth.
I don't remember details of dreams much anymore,
but this one was still vivid.

The pig was laid out on the table,
and I helped myself to it.
The skin was crisp and the
meat was succulent.
It was so damn tender you didn't even
need to chew it, it just melted.

I took the carving knife and fork and
moved to the pig's head and sliced off
a fleshy part of the cheek.
While I ate it, I looked at the pig's face and
I saw tears rolling down from its
shut eyes, down its now mutilated cheek to
the bright red apple in its mouth.

I found these details slightly disturbing and
a little disconcerting,
and thought it best not to
delve too deep into why,
besides the obvious,
that the pig was crying.

Just Another Autumn Day

The tea I made is hot and soothing
(Earl Grey, with a teaspoon of
milk and honey).

I open the windows to let in
the cool, chilling breeze
(fifty-seven degrees, and rain outside)

I sit, in cross legged Indian style,
on my recliner
(swaddled in the quilt I received
last Christmas).

The music I choose it fitting
(Autumn Jazz, the playlist
on my phone says).

I close my eyes to the sounds of
soft piano and a saxophonist who
plays as if he understands
all that ever was and will be.

My conscience is as clear as it's ever been,
and would that the Lord would take
me now while it still is.

One One-Thousand, Two One-Thousand, Three

I sit on my couch on this dreary morning and
watch out the window the rain falling in droves.
I finish my first cup of black coffee,
which is way too bitter.
Serves me right for cheapening out and
buying the store-brand rotgut.

Once my cup is drained, I stare into it for far
too long, and I decide I can't take it anymore.
I rise and go to the kitchen to pour a second cup,
store -brand rotgut be damned.

After I fill my mug again with crap coffee,
I turn from the coffee maker and start
towards the liquor cabinet to grab what
remains of my bottle of Jameson.
I unscrew the cap and pour.

One one-thousand,
two one-thousand,
three.

I take a big sip,
then continue to think of her,
as I have every morning this autumn
since she left.
Autumn was our season,
hers and mine...
                    ...not *his*

Now I think of him and her and
what they do together.
What she told me they did the other
night, because I'm stupid and I'm
a caveman and I was insistent on knowing.

Damn her. Damn him. Damn them.

And damn me most of all.

Indian Corn

There was a display of Indian corn in the
Autumn section of Walmart the other day and
before I knew it I was back at my
grandmother's old house when
I was four years old and we used to live there.

Sittoo, why are you hanging brown corn?

> *It's Indian corn, Sweetheart.*

Can you eat it?

> *No dear, it's for decoration, like the Jack-O'- Lantern
> you carved with Mommy earlier.*

Can you make popcorn out of it?

> *No honey, you can't.*

Can you play with it?

> *If you used your imagination, I'm sure you could.*

Did the Indians play with it?

> *I'm sure they did.*

Can you put it on a rocket to the Moon?

> *I'm sure you could sweetie.*

Why is it hard and brown?

> *Sweetheart don't you have something to color or
> play with somewhere else? Sittoo's a little busy.*

When I was back in the present,
I decided to buy some without hesitation.

This one's for you Sittoo, I say,
as I hang it on my front door and
admire it with a smile before
going back inside.

A Perfect Day, I Dare Say

The rain outside today falls gently,
peacefully, quietly, like it's hardly even there,
like you'd imagine it would at a Shinto Shrine.
The weatherman says showers all day.
I have an autumn scented candle lit (*Autumn Walk*)
so the apartment can smell and have a cozy feel to it,
a mug of black coffee with a full pot still on,
and a collection of ghost stories I bought a few
years ago that I've regrettably not yet read.

Why not now?
It's a fine day for it.
A perfect day, I dare say.

I dared to speak too soon.

Three pages in and,
wouldn't you know it,
wouldn't you God damn know it,
I start thinking of you.
You and the fact no matter how obviously perfect
we'd be together, you just refuse to see it and
remain steadfast in your rejection.

I close the book and my eyes and
let out an exasperated sigh.

Why do you always do this to yourself,
the voice asks me.

Because I'm a bumbling idiot,
is the only honest response I have.

Hearth and Home

Baby, I know I don't wax poetic to your
face but that's because I'd feel like
a complete and utter doofus.
So I tell you on paper like
Jim Croce told his wife I love you in a song.

You know you're the cold gin on my porch
after work on a hot summer day.

You know you're the comforting silence from my
backyard during a heavy snowfall.

You know you're the scent of my mother's
oatmeal cookies returning home from
football practice on a crisp fall night with an aching body.

And you know damn well you're my place of comfort,
my place of warmth and welcome.
My hearth and home,
and I'll return for as long as
you keep the door open.

I don't *need* to tell you this,
but I love your smile when I do.

Through the Eyes of Paul Newman

He sees himself in the bathroom mirror
before he's had his morning coffee and
splashed ice cold water on his face.

He stares deep into the reflection,
A stare of revulsion, of hate, of pity.

How different our life would be,
he says to the reflection,
had we been blessed with blue eyes instead of brown.
Why could we not stare back at us
through the eyes of Paul Newman?
Rather than through eyes the color of mud and shit.

He finally splashes his face with cold water,
and with a sigh of annoyance,
inconvenience, and defeat,
goes out to meet his day.

Utility Bowl

Have you ever been so lazy that
you used the unwashed bowl
with dried soup still stuck to its sides for cereal?

Then, used the same unwashed bowl,
now caked with dried milk,
for soup again?
Probably later that same day?

I have.
Many times.
Many, many times.

And I don't know what to
do to change that.

Beer is For Me

I thrice tap the beer can before
cracking it, and the dog,
who's been lying on her bed peacefully,
perks her head and ears up,
selfishly thinking it's for her.

No silly, I say,
beer is not for you.

Her head tilts and she raises her brow
inquisitively to show curiousness in
her brown, almond-shaped eyes.

No, I repeat, beer is for me.
I sip deep and gulp heavy,
for sorry pieces of shit like me.

Masterpiece

She sleeps tonight uncovered,
turned over on her side.
Pale moonlight through the windows
illuminates her legs.
The teardrop of her thighs,
the defined muscles of her calves,
the dips and turns about her ankles,
the smoothed roundness of her heels.

My body trembles as my fingers
softly glide along and trace the
masterpiece I've just described —
glowing silver marble reflected in the night.

Neon-Tinted Rabbit Hole

The edible now has me fully in its grasp.
Blankly, I stare far off and see a
ceaselessly spinning vortex of every color in the prism.

Reds and yellows,
greens and blues and everything in between.
A shimmering rotation stretching towards infinity beyond.

Through a cosmic sort of haze I see them laughing,
gathered 'round merry tables without me.
No longer wanted,
no longer needed.
Out of sight and mind together.

That's okay though,
because I see past them and into
the neon-tinted rabbit hole.

I am happy here.
It is here I feel I am forever welcome and
where I choose to stay.

It is here that I see all,
know all.
am all.

Ruminating on My Thirty-Second Birthday

As the sun begins setting on my
thirty-second year and thirty-three prepares to rise,
it is my firm belief that
the most important of the
many lessons learned this
year was this—

Take nothing to your grave.

A Girl He Really Liked

He was halfway through his second bottle
of wine on what we all know as "one of those nights,"
when he, for no real reason,
and much to his chagrin,
remembered that one time years ago when a
girl he really liked fucked one of his
best buddies and they kept it a secret for
months until during one of
the gangs many nights out,
a drunken slip-of-the-tongue from his other
buddy revealed the
truth and he had to leave the bar so
no one would see him cry.

Had it been some random floozy and not the
girl he sat next to in Italian all year who would
give him gum if he needed it and even took
a sip of his spiked coffee one morning,
who he bought a brand of beer for
she thought could only be found where she was
from in Queens as a nice, friendly gesture,
he probably would not have felt like the
Kong-sized pile of shit he now realized
he was in the eyes of people who called
themselves his friends.

His friend said he was sorry and regretted
it and that's why he didn't say anything.
He chose to believe it,
women trip and land on erect cocks all
the time after all.

What else could he do?

This was his circle, and he was a loyal soldier.
But it was a hard way to learn that loyalty was
more often than not the most disposable of virtues.

What a proud moment for me,
he muttered to himself as he took
another very deep swig from the wine bottle,
what a good friend I was.

New Years, 2019

Tonight, I ring in the New Year alone.
No woman around.
No Friends.
No Family.

Alone.

Alone and in the shower.
First shower in four days because it
was clogged and full of tepid filth water all week.
But it's clogged no more and drains freely.

Fare thee well, grime.
Fare thee well, Twenty-Eighteen.

My first shower of the new year finds me
ringin' it in with a clean conscience and
a clean nutsack.

Hahahahaha and just like that,
as I dry off,
I am inspired,
as if touched by Divine Providence—

> May your taints not smell sour,
> May your scrotums have sheen,
> May you be blessed with
> a squeaky clean Twenty-Nineteen

Up to the Moon

She bitched to me one night that
she was never my first choice and
I wanted to scream at the top of
my lungs to her that she was right.

I wanted to scream to her,
to drill into her fat fucking obnoxious head that
she wouldn't have been my second, third,
or forth choice either if
not for the fact she had her tits pushed up to
the moon the night I met her and
I was way, way too drunk to say no.

Cleavage, a low cut shirt,
cheap booze, and raging hormones was
how my last choice morphed into
the only choice I had left.

What the Hell For?

Sometimes, he began to himself,
sitting in his recliner all alone in his
apartment, boxer shorts riding up the
crack of his ass and likely accumulating shit stains,
he said to himself,
Sometimes I'd really like the last
ten years of my life back.

> *What the hell for?* he heard a voice answer,
> *So you could know different people?*
> *Have a different job?*
> *Live in a different place?*
> *Have dated different women?*
> *Then come home to sit where you are*
> *now and stick your hand down your*
> *shit-stained boxers to scratch your*
> *balls like you're doing now?*

Well, he replied,
when you put it like that...

On the Cusp of Midnight

Call it a night, the party's over,
and tomorrow starts the same old thing again.
-Willie Nelson

I

Every Friday night,
right about the time Friday becomes Saturday,
I hear her footsteps coming up the stairs to my door,
I see her walk in without knocking,
her vintage leather jacket thrown over her
shoulder like Sinatra, before being thrown over
my kitchen chair like she owned the
place and she'd snap her fingers asking,
with wry, bossy smile at the ready.
Where's my vodka cran, darling?

The good times don't often last though,
and in this case someone else came along for her.
It's now pushing two years since
her footsteps climbed my stairs,
since she opened my door without knocking,
since her jacket was on my chair,
since I saw her face in person.

But it hasn't been that long since I made
a strong vodka cran,
which I make every Friday on the
cusp of midnight just before we
welcome Saturday to the fold.

It brings her back to me, you see,
makes those cold Friday nights of mine,
like the one's she once held dominion over,
a little less lonely,
and I try to sip it slow so she
doesn't run out of here too fast.
It's a long haul, getting to the next Friday.

II

I made another vodka cran for her tonight.
This one though, I didn't make with the
intention of keeping her with me.
This one I slowly poured into the sink.
You know me,
you know just how God damned
hard that was for me to do.

It felt as though some presence was wrestling with
my hand before I turned the glass over.
It physically hurt,
and I felt nauseous doing it.
But, in one of those rare times I was seeing clearly,
I knew what needed doing.

When that last drop had dripped from the glass,
and all the sanguine-colored liquor found
its way down the drain,
I turned over the glass and gently set it
on the kitchen table,
and that's where it'll stay until her ghost
no longer haunts my midnights.

The Neighbor Kids and a Ladybug

I've chosen, today, to give up.
It seems like an odd day to call it quits —
a bright Wednesday afternoon, seventy degrees with
a soft summer breeze just strong enough
to rustle a few trees.

Maybe it doesn't seem like such an odd day after all,
maybe it's the perfect day to call it quits.

From my seat on the porch,
contemplating all this,
I see the neighbor kids across the street playing
some pickup basketball with their father in
their driveway court.
They do this on the daily in the summer,
and in truth it's kind of fun to watch.

I hope the neighbor kids decide
to never give up like I have.
We were all neighbor kids playing
basketball with our dads for a time.
I pray nothing ever leads them to where I am.

A very strong gust of wind surges
and knocks my hat off.
After I curse and the wind dies,
a ladybug lands and rests on my right hand.
I let her crawl, and watch her fly away.
I decided at that moment I'm
not calling it quits today.

Holes in the Crotch

I work hard for what I have —
I make rent every month,
I don't miss my car payments,
and I haven't starved yet.

Why then, after my fourth thirteen-hour
day in a row, do I sit in my recliner with
no lights on, no TV on, no music on,
staring at and through the wall to the
Great Beyond wearing nothing but my underwear
feeling unfulfilled and worthless?

I have my answer when I see the
three empty pizza boxes on the floor,
next to the two pairs of
underwear, all with holes or the beginnings
of holes in the crotch,
which lie next to a rather embarrassingly
large mound of crusty socks,
also with holes in them.

As Ancient as Methuselah

The heat wave, that sweltering, sweltering
heat wave that made it too hot to swim and
never seemed to want to end, finally broke today.
The sky turned a dark grey, almost black,
and opened up, letting loose her
sorrow in a torrent that went all day.

I pull into my parking spot at
home after a busy work day in a long
string of consecutive days working
both the day and the night job.

But there's no work tonight at least.
No sir.
Finally. I can breathe.
I shut the engine off and listen to
the heavy pitter patter of the rain bouncing
off the roof and windshield of my car.
So strong and constant it becomes a heavy drone.

A thin, weary smile crosses my face.
I hear a rumble of thunder roll across the
valley that feels as ancient as Methuselah.

The afternoon is mine to do with as I please.
As is tomorrow.
As is this month.
As is this life.

Crack of a Bat at Fenway

It feels like an eternity since I got to
sit on the porch in my Adirondack chair.
My coffee and a book at the ready.
It's like meeting up with a friend you
haven't seen in ages and it feels no time's passed.

The summer has been a brutal one—
sixty-hour work weeks, high heat,
cloudless skies, high humidity, heavy, monsoon type
rain that traps you inside your home while not
cooling things off a single degree.
I haven't had time to properly meditate
here in my place of peace.

Today I reclaim my Garden of Eden.
The temperature is just over seventy with
no humidity to speak of,
the air is fresh and crisp.

The breeze comes from the north and brings with
it just the right cloud cover to make you believe
you just heard the crack of a bat at
Fenway if you shut your eyes.
I can almost smell the sausage and
peppers all the way from Boston now.

I'm going to love this day.
It's not even a question of if,
but to a matter of degrees.
Even if all I accomplish today is
a hundred or so pages read and my
ass falling asleep in my chair.

Secrets of the World

I wanted to walk with her on
cold and rainy autumn mornings in
the woods that surrounded her property,
with nothing but the sounds of
raindrops and our footsteps on
the wet and fallen orange leaves in our ears.

When I was a boy I would walk the
woods by my grandmother's on days like this,
I knew the trail there like the back of my
hand and the loneliness was more blessing than burden.

Dry in my yellow raincoat and muckboots,
I'd wander with no one but myself and my imagination,
with no one but the Gods of Rain and Forest watching on.

I wanted to bring that wonder to her in
the early morning autumn rain,
the truths and mysteries I've discovered,
and to share with her all the secrets of
the world I've learned that haven't
yet ceased to amaze me.

November

I ever tell you how you remind me of November?

Grey clouds hang low with the slow,
encroaching chill of winter's first bite.

The sun sets before supper time as
early darkness greets us merrily.

Rain becomes wet snow mid-descent,
wood smoke can be smelt on the air,
thermostats are turned up,
and a welcoming warmth embraces us
as we come inside from out.

The urge to nap overtakes us as
the kettle brews for tea and
coffee pots are filled.

Stew simmers in the slow cooker;
casseroles bake in the oven.

Dark and cold. Comfort and warmth.
Beautiful dark and beautiful comfort.
Beautiful cold and beautiful warmth.

I'm sorry if I hadn't told you that before,
but trust me, being November is one of the best
things you can ever be.

Worth It?

She was nothing more
    than a perfect set
of legs and for
    so long they were
all mine to savor.

        All it cost me
            was a handful of
      years, my dignity, and
         all my self-respect.

Scars

That one?
This one smelled of cucumber melon —
as deep and inviting as her
eyes were green and generous.

And this one?
Cigarettes and Red Bull.
Where is the appeal in that, one might wonder.
Just like her and the red flannel she wore,
it was raw, it was earthy, it was real.

And what about her?
I wish you hadn't made me recall this one.
Fresh as the day she was born,
the essence of mist off of cascading falls.

And her?
Dark. So dark.
Burnt leaves and
late night October rain.

It's the only proof of their existence,
the scents that remain like so many scars.

And when the scent is gone?
I will wail and weep,
and be thankful later for their parting.

For the Pooch

Alert gremlin ears and
the wag of that tail says a lot.
It tells me—

Never shall I lie.
Never shall I mislead.
Never shall I be insincere.
Never shall I guide you astray.
Never shall I tire of the sight of you.

Same goes for me, poochy,
same goes for me.

Termination

If the arithmetic was correct,
he went over in his head the
other day for no discernible reason,
the child, had there been no termination,
would be roughly two and a half right now.

He knew he was in no position to
cast the first stone,
but he could never quite be certain that,
before she made the decision that she did,
she knew who the father was.
And through this uncertainty, no one was sure.

He wondered too if,
for the past two and a half years,
did the child visit her every night in her
sleep just as it had visited him.

The Drive Into Work

It's a rainy morning on his drive
into work today.
He's reminded of all the other early morning
drives he once had that were exceedingly more
painful than his current trip,
crying and screaming and cursing his life.

Working, slaving away at rail yards or
warehouses where he'd break both body and
soul in rain, snow, ice, and wind.
Or in heat and dust and grime for
the faceless corporate overseers that
wouldn't piss on him were he on fire.

> That isn't my life anymore,
> he says proudly,
> and it never will be again.

He gets to, every morning now,
chop lettuce and prep chicken and
beans for the day's coming business.
The money isn't great,
and some naysayers would say he's taken
a step back, and maybe in a way he has,

> But that doesn't mean a damn to me,
> They're jealous and won't admit it because,
> unlike them,
> I'm no longer sobbing on the drive
> into work anymore.

*Disclaimer

Some places I go are filled with laughter,
joy, and tenderness.
I like writing about childhood or my parents or
smokes and drinks and food and basketball.
And when I'm finished,
the heart thrives in a state of elation,
of warmth, and lifted spirits.

You may feel the same if you
come with me on that journey.

However,
be forewarned.

Some places I go are dark,
are evil and disturbing.
There I willingly and unrepentantly walk with
demons and maliciously grinning devils that frighten me,
and give me pause to wonder just who and what I am.

You may feel the same,
if you come on this journey too.

Do not look at me in disgust or
judge me in your horror.
I go where I go and travel where
I wish and where you dare
not to because I am human and am unafraid to.

And, because I am human,
I dare to say I like it.

Like Poor Steve McQueen

"I was home. What happened? What the hell happened?"
*-Steve McQueen, at the end of **The Sand Pebbles***

Woke up drooling into my pillow and
with a splitting headache after working
my latest fourteen hour day.
I stumbled over my laundry pile which was
actually my *dog* laying on my laundry pile,
to the kitchen where I stepped on a pizza box that
fell off the edge of the counter overnight.
I saw it, but I'm not full of enough care to pick it up.

I put the coffee on and poured a cup before
I walked away to take a piss.
I pissed with morning wood at half mast,
so the mess was minimal.

I shuffled to the recliner and sat on a
stale tortilla chip I debated eating for a
good five seconds before deciding I'm
too classy to do that.

I noticed I've been in the buff this
entire time and put on a pair of
underwear I get from the dog's laundry
pile I had previously stumbled over.

I curse myself for having forgotten about
my coffee and go back to the kitchen for
it and step on the pizza box again which I
disgustingly just slide out of my field of
vision under the kitchen table.

I currently stand in the kitchen in my
old pair of saggy underwear sipping lukewarm
coffee, and I ask myself out loud when the hell I'll
be able to, or if I'm even capable of,
getting my life together.

Hopefully I can,
before the next question
comes too late and I curse myself like
poor Steve McQueen at the end of
The Sand Pebbles before getting gunned down.

The Last Son of Krypton

We almost lost you last year when
you passed out at the wheel and
rolled a handful of times into a field where
luckily there were no trees to hit
or ponds to drown in.

To this day you still insist it was due to bad
popcorn you ate at the movies and not
on the fact you had just finished a
six-thousand mile road trip in less than a week.

That's the first and only time I
ever saw you scared —
hooked up to IV's and machines in
the ER bed not knowing why in
Christ's name you were there.
You're human just like the rest of us,
that's why you were there.

Yes, somehow you escaped a rollover with
nothing but a black eye from an errant
golf ball smacking you in the face.
Yes, you easily run six miles a
day and hike almost every other.

Yes, you're healthier and look better than
most men half your age and you'll
probably outlive *me* and hell that's a
testament to yourself.

But, contrary to what you believe,
you are in fact *not* the Last Son of Krypton.
You're retired, take it just a little easy.
You're the only Dad we got,
and there's still many miles to
go and many putts to sink.

How I'm Doing

When I'm asked by my
coworkers each day how
I'm doing and I
respond with ho-hum
nonchalance that I don't
really want to be here today —

I wonder if any of them
have picked up on
what I mean by "Here."

Capital G

I had a hunch I'd have to say
goodbye to you some day.
A real, sad, solid goodbye.
The sort of goodbye that doesn't
mean *See ya later* or *Until next time*.
The sort of goodbye that means
Goodbye, capital G and all.
The sort of goodbye reserved for
those doomed from the start.

With the September sun shining and
a slight breeze to make this already
crisp morning even cooler,
this seems like as good a day as
any to get that over and done with.
I should be able to live with that
easy after the tears are shed and
the curses are shouted.

End Scene

It baffles me how many times
up to this point that
I've wanted to
shut my eyes and call it
a life but I always think
to myself Oh what the hell
I may as well see this
play through until *finis scaena*
and take my final bow
during the curtain call.

A Farewell That Didn't Kill Me

And if that really was the last time—
lying together naked on a bitter,
frigid winter's night with only the
comforter and our body heat keeping us warm,
listening to Cash and Dylan serenade us about
the girl from where the winds hit
heavy on the borderline—
well, Love, let me tell you,
I've had farewells far, far
worse than the one we just shared.

I'm Doing Well, Actually

How am I feeling lately?
Well, since you asked —

I'm doing well, actually.
So well in fact that I'm no
longer sleeping with cookie crumbs that
fall from my chest to the bed sheets when
I eat cookies in bed.

I was very sad during that period.

Now, when I stay in bed all day and
eat three full sleeves of Dollar Tree
vanilla crèmes, I sweep those silly
crumbs away in one confident,
fluid motion right onto the floor next to my
books, my unwashed underwear,
my hopes and dreams, and a new layer of dust.

The Sardonic Voice of Zevon

It's the worst kind of late March morning.
I went to bed to the pitter patter of
rain in my ears and woke up to
twenty-degree temperatures and
three-inches of sloppy, wet, heavy snow.

I shuffle slowly to the bathroom,
still dazed from last night's gin and
lack of sleep. I rinse out the cottonmouth
with cold water and splash it on my
face but it neither freshens,
wakes, or sobers.

Looking into the mirror at this
heavy eyed, disheveled face I can't
believe is mine, I sigh and shake my head.
Tomorrow starts another tough work week.
Both jobs five days in a row.
Another week of straight doubles.

The face in the mirror asks why
I keep doing this to myself.
I ponder this for a moment before
the sardonic voice of Zevon
prances through my head

> So much to do,
> there's plenty on the farm.

I'll sleep when I'm dead,
I sing to my reflection,
I'll sleep when I'm dead.

Top Shelf

I barely paid the minimum on
my credit card yesterday,
he says to her from across the table,
but here I sit with you at a restaurant
I can't afford regularly, with my
four-hundred dollar Swiss watch on
my wrist, wearing a Ralph Lauren sweater,
Jos. A Bank dress boots, and there's
top-shelf gin in this martini.

He took a deep sip from his
aforementioned top-shelf martini,
then he reached across and took her hand in his.

I'm nervous as shit, every day,
of falling into that pit.
Afraid that my future will be terrible.
That anything good that happens has a
price to pay the piper later.

But hell, beautiful, sometimes you
have to know when to throw
caution to the wind and say
Fuck it, today I God damn live.

He sipped his martini again,
and she sipped hers,
and she looked at him in a
way that made him think she
was the first person to believe in him.

It Isn't Hers Anymore Now Anyway

Christ almighty, he thought to himself as
his mother and sister continued going
through his grandmother's closet in her bedroom.
The bedroom, he thought, it isn't hers anymore now anyway,
and he hated himself for thinking that.

He looked around and concluded that there
was nothing more sad, surreal, or empty feeling as
a fully furnished and decorated living space
to which someone would never return.

A chair in front of the small TV would
no longer be used to watch Federer
at Wimbledon that year.

A knitting kit that will miss
the touch of familiar hands.
A small Mr. Coffee on the
counter, by a small toaster,
that wouldn't brew another cup or
make another piece of toast.

Pictures of friends and family on the
walls that won't be looked at again from
the perspective of the person who hung them.
The memories of these people,
both familiar and unknown,
will leave the Earth with her.

The collage for her that his little cousin made
in school when she was eight,
I Love Grandma it said in big
glitter letters with cut out and
pasted pictures of the past decade behind glass.
A beautiful declaration of love that
means nothing to no one now.

He heard his mother begin to
cry from the bedroom,
with his sister trying to comfort her.

Fuck, he whispered,
and let out a very heavy sigh before
heading over to comfort her too.

We Need to Talk About Bullying

They had him cornered in the
bathroom by the computer lab.
Fucking little bitch, they called him.
Pussy, faggot, and retard too.

Leave me the fuck alone, he said back,
trying to muster courage and defiance but
feeling his body on the verge of trembling
from the nerves rising from the pit of his stomach.

He tried to shove them out of the way
towards the door but there were too many,
his only hope was for someone who wasn't a
piece of shit to walk in and break it up.

Haha you fat faggot, they said laughing,
he thinks he's a fuckin' tough guy.
You a badass? Another one said, huh?
A real big badass?

These were the lowlifes who would either
drop out in another year or so,
were sophomores or juniors who
had been held back once or twice,
or skip so much that you forgot they even existed.
He knew who they were,
everyone knew who everyone was at
least by sight in a school of four hundred,
and even though they were strangers to each other,
he knew why they had chosen to target him.

They were the older kids,
wannabe street toughs in a small rural town nestled
in Nowhere, New York,
and he was the chubby freshman who dyed his
hair purple and wore his Korn and Metallica shirts and
ripped jeans with Chuck Taylors to school.
He was a quiet, friendly, shy kid who

just wanted to be left alone the majority of the time.

Unbeknownst to them,
he also played offensive line for
the freshman football team,
and he knew how to both hit and take a hit,
and the angrier he got the less the
rules that govern the fabric and civility of
society mattered to him.

While they shoved him and smacked the
back of his head and continued in their belittling,
he remembered the pen in the right pocket of his jeans.
He reached in, took it out, clicked it,
and in his rage with a yell he stabbed their leader just
below his ribs. He yelped out in pain.
The fucking faggot just stabbed me! he yelled.
I'm gonna kill you now fatass! the leader yelled

They started punching him but they were
weak punches and he felt nothing,
nothing but hate.
Pure hate.
A deep, dark, animalistic hate he
reserved only for the gridiron.

In his hatred he wrapped his hands around
the leaders neck and began squeezing,
growling like a beast, looking the leader in the
eyes as the other two cronies kept hitting him and
tried to pull him away.
He felt tears in his eyes and a burning rage
as he shouted *I hate you* and *I hope you die.*

That last one scared him,
not because he had yelled it,
but because he hadn't thought twice about it,
and thought that maybe he had meant it.

He knew if caught, he would be the one suspended.

Justice in public school serves not the tormented,
and because of that he didn't believe he'd have sobbed over
the loss of his tormentor's life.
He was thirteen years old,
he just wanted to be left alone,
and he had just sincerely wanted someone
to die by his hand.

We're Better Than That, Beautiful

I don't need to mention setting
suns or moons and stars and
rainbows and rivers of crystal clear bullshit when
talking about you or how much I
love and adore you.

I don't need to peruse the Thesaurus for
ten-dollar superfluous words only a
stuffy academic would understand to
describe this and that and you and me.

Who am I trying to impress?
The outside world?
Piss on the outside world and everyone in it.
This is for us.
For you and me and that is it.

You and I don't need pretentious piffle.
The two of us?
We're better than that, beautiful.
For always and ever or for as long as you
can stand me—
we'll be better than that.

Heathen

You haven't fully lived until you've
bought the gang a round and proceeded to
dance like a bumbling fucking fool while
double-fisting High Life and laughing so hard
it hurts the moment before you black out.

It was ten in the morning and that's what her
older brother proclaimed immediately after
walking through the door.

And where exactly, she asked, sipping her
coffee while preparing to finish
knitting the scarf she had been working on,
are your pants?

He looked down at his lower half,
on which he currently wore only his
black Chuck Taylors and his ghastly
orange boxer briefs.

Well, he began, *I pissed myself sometime*
during the night, so obviously I threw them in the wash.

You drove all the way back here from
Steve's house wearing your cold,
piss-soaked pants when it's twenty outside?

Goodness no, he said, almost offended
she would even consider he'd do that,
I took them off before I left.

You drove back here in just your sweatshirt and
boxer briefs? she asked surprised,
but not really at all surprised.

Yes, he said, looking down at his bare legs,
Yes I did. But at least I didn't soil his
couch this time, one screaming match
with that girlfriend of his is more than

enough for this lifetime.

She just stared at him.

You're a heathen, she said, shaking her head

Yes, he said with a smile, *yes I am.*

Should I Call In?

There's a good, heavy late March rain
coming down outside.
I've been awake for five hours and
have to leave for work in ten minutes.

It's ten of one in the afternoon,
on a Friday, and I've yet to change out of
my crappy PJ's or even turn on a light.
Should I call in?
Sit and sip some more coffee?
Eat some pizza while sitting in
the dark alone and in my underwear?

I could read something?
Maybe pound off?
Maybe write something?
Maybe watch some basketball and
nap next to the pooch?
Literally every option is a better
option than going to that place on a
dreary, rainy late Friday afternoon.

That's where I'm at right now —
I have the chance to not do a single productive thing at
all and fuck yourself if you're judging me for craving it.

I've made my decision,
and begin working on my sick voice
before making the call.

Suit Up for the Yankees

I find myself waking up at 3:37 in the morning
despite the fact I don't have to be up for work until 6.
This is it; I know I'm not getting back to sleep.
I'm warm under my comforter, but I can see,
from the frost that's accrued on the windows,
that it's a clear night and bitter cold outside.

For whatever reason, my thoughts turn to
that of old Mrs. Lindenhaur,
who played the organ at the church I went to as a kid.
I remember how she and my grandmother would
gab before service would begin in that way old
church ladies gab, and how she always wore the
smile you only see from said old church-going ladies.
I'm not entirely sure that smile exists anymore,
I believe it has fled this world like the
sounds and smells of springs and summers past.

While waiting for my grandmother to
finish talking, which felt like eternity to an eight year old,
Mrs. Lindenhaur's white haired but
no less strapping husband, Owen,
would come join the conversation and, upon noticing me,
would shake my hand and call me young man and
ask when I'd be ready to suit up for the Yankees.

His hands were strong and rough but gentle,
and I've never known what he did for a living.
He was every bit the older gentleman —
a perfectly trimmed, snow white mustache and beard,
a dark brown herringbone blazer, a gold pocket watch
in his matching vest,
he even walked occasionally with a squire's cane.
As service would begin and we'd part for
our seats he would muss my hair and
wish us many blessings for the day and week.

I'm so overtired it hurts and I'm
hovering between sleep and consciousnesses.
I don't know what's real and what isn't anymore,
but I unexpectedly find very real tears in
my eyes for the late Lindenhaurs,
and I hear myself whispering an apology
to Owen for never having suited up for the Yankees.

The Mask of Shame I Wear

"I am tomorrow, or some future day,
what I establish today. I am today what
I established yesterday or some previous day."
-James Joyce

My hopes and dreams and goals are not hard to explain,
and always come back to the same two
distinct but, but very different aspirations.

On one hand, I dream of a day that dawns where I
bedeck my wrist with a differing luxury watch a day,
have a walk in closest chock full of
designer suits and shoes that I'll wear
to The Bohemian Club where I'll sit in a
leather wing-back armchair and savor the
taste of top-shelf whiskey and gin,
smoke only the finest cigars,
and bask in the general glow of fulfillment at
having achieved such a Herculean triumph,
having come from humble, small town origins.
The son of a toll collector and an
electric company meter man,
I shouldn't know what a
Rolex even looks like.

But,
the yin to my yang and the devil to my angel,
on the other hand,
I fall victim to my own sloth time and time again,
and very much would like to go about my
days in some ensemble of sweatpants or
gym shorts with a matching crap sweatshirt
that's likely stained with yesterday's
pizza or the remnants of my children
who never were as I move from bed to
couch to toilet.
Rinse and Repeat.
On second thought the toilet is optional,

I'll piss off the porch.

But to live every day like that?
In stained sweatpants?
After a while would it would not be
my sad and sorry reflection I'd see in the mirror.
I would be hidden behind the
mask of shame I wear to hide my true face.

The face of defeat.
The face of cowardice.
My eyes would reveal I had played it safe and free of risk.
That I had deserted the pursuit of
higher actualization, and even worse,
that I had accepted it.

What, then, am I to do?
I could, and very likely will, fall on my face and
fail miserably in the pursuit of becoming the
Me of my adulthood dreams,
and still end my days a shamefully masked reflection
bedecked in stained and soiled sweatpants.

But I could at least give it an honest to God shot.
I'd like to cross the veil knowing I had tried.
That I didn't just bend over and
willingly take failure deep and hard and raw.
I don't want to hang up my cleats and accept that
this is my life now and there's nothing more to it.

I want my shot at the wing-back chair and
the top-shelf liquor and the designer suits and
the Bohemian Club and the finest cigars.

Piss on failure.

This pursuit ends with a final image and final
fuck you and farewell to a life lived in
squalor, worry, and despair.

A final goodbye to sleeping on couches and
mattresses with no box spring and using
books and pillows as plates and drinking
Mad Dog and Wild Irish Rose and
ramen or rice for dinner every night and
not affording jeans and new shoes.

This pursuit ends with a glistening timepiece wrapped
around and resting comfortably on my wrist,
and an outlandishly priced Churchill clenched between
the teeth of a laughing devil's grin,
from which smoke will dance towards
the sky to greet the Gods hello from me.

Also From G.M. Manzi

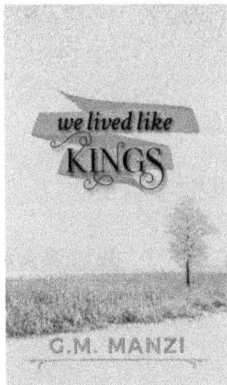

"I'd one day love to spin a tale from yarn weaved from that which brings me joy, peace, and serenity. But the fount of creativity is unfortunately better fed by the spring from which flow my miseries, misfortunes, and unforgiving hatreds."

G.M. Manzi ruminates the everyday introspection without sugarcoating or special dressing. Read like a friend sharing from his heart on a muggy summer evening in the back yard, pipe in hand, mesmerized by the rising smoke and long pauses between thoughts. He counters rough memories with softer moments and hindsight. Sit back, prop up your feet, and soak in the significant minutes.

About the Author

G.M. Manzi is an independent author for fun and grocery store butcher by trade residing in New York's Capitol District with his loyal pooch Tatty. His hobbies are relaxing on the porch and enjoying the occasional martini. He still has no plans to take up camping. He is not the recipient of any awards or fellowships but this doesn't stop him from telling himself everyday that the cream always rises eventually. He is the author of *We Lived Like Kings*.

www.ingramcontent.com/pod-product-compliance
Lightning Source LLC
Chambersburg PA
CBHW032019090426
42741CB00006B/667